THE MEMOIR MIDWIFE®

Nine Steps to Self-Publishing Your Book
(Second Edition)

To Michele,
Thank you so
much for your
fabulous reviews!
Share your Stories
with the world!
xoxo,

Stacy

Cheers for
NINE STEPS

When Stacy and I started working together, I had no idea that publishing a book was so complex. Her guidance was the difference between my book sitting in a folder on my hard drive, and it actually getting published in both English and Spanish, hard copies, Kindle, you name it!

- *Kirsten Henry Fox Author of* THE PROFITABLE WINE LIST: Three Steps to Quickly & Easily Increase Wine Sales

Dymalski takes all of those intimidating elements of self-publishing and breaks them down, giving you a step-by-step on how to get your book into the world. I've self-published a series, but learned more from this gem of a guide than I could have imagined. BISAC, POD, ISBN, Library of Congress, EIN, handling finances, design and production, she covers it all. And with her trademark wit, Stacy is both entertaining and encouraging along the way. I highly recommend this guide for anyone considering taking their words to the world. (Note: I found this because I love her book *Confessions of a Band Geek Mom*. If you haven't read it, it's a riot.)

- *Amanda Turner, author of* Vagabonding With Kids

With Stacy's help and her amazing book, I finished and published my own book in three months. Her money saving tips add even more value, which clearly makes her book worth much more than the price. I continue to learn from her via her online courses and workshops as I venture into writing my second book.

- *Shiral Torres, author of* Rental Properties Made Simple: A No-Nonsense Straightforward Guide to Managing Your Rental Properties

I have self-published one book already before reading this one, but got valuable tips of steps that I had skipped or did not think of. Stacy uses her wit and humor to explain the self-publishing process in an easy-to-understand and entertaining way. I especially liked the step-by-step approach and the extra tips at the end of each step. It is everything you need to successfully self-publish your book. Now I am just waiting for a follow up book, with the marketing tips she taught in her course too.

  - Tess Whitty, author of Marketing Tips for Translators

I was so bewildered with all the things that self-publishing involved and then I bought this book. Stacy breaks it down and provides a concise checklist with great explanations of terms and why you should or should not do something. And she isn't kidding when she says to hire experts! That saved me so much time and frustration!

  - Karen, Amazon Review

After reading my husband's copy of this book, I ordered one to send to a friend who is self-publishing this time around after a bad experience with the publisher of his first book. Stacy's book is a clear, concise blueprint on how to take control of your publishing experience. Highly recommended for both aspiring and established authors.

  - Robin Garreaud, Amazon Review

This was a great, quick read that provided all the nuggets I was looking for in the world of self-publishing! The Memoir Midwife breaks down self-publishing as easy and attainable. Now that I know where to start, I can get busy!

  - Sarah Dalling, Amazon Review

THE MEMOIR MIDWIFE®

Nine Steps to Self-Publishing Your Book
(Second Edition)

All new updated information on the easiest
and fastest way to self-publish your book!

By Stacy Dymalski

Saffire Press
Park City, Utah

Published in the United States by Saffire Press
PO Box 2507, Park City, UT 84060

The Memoir Midwife®:
Nine Steps to Self-Publishing Your Book, Second Edition

Library of Congress Control Number (LCCN):2019912152
ISBN: 978-0-9909775-2-0

Printed in the United States of America

Interior design by Katie Mullaly of Surrogate Press®
Cover design by Michelle Rayner of Cosmic Design
Brand elements and character art created by
Ali Wright of Dapper Fox Design
Back cover photo by Liz Barlak of Liz Barlak Photography

To my sons, Derrick and Quinn,

You inspire me every day to push the limits.
Mainly because over the course of raising
you, you've pushed my limits.
But that's another story.

- Mom -

To aspiring authors,

What the heck are you waiting for?
Get out there and write that book.
Now that the traditional publishing gatekeepers
are gone, there's nothing stopping you…
…except yourself.

- S.D. -

Other Books by Stacy Dymalski

Confessions of a Band Geek Mom
(One Exhausted Parent's Take on Carpools, Room Mothers,
High School Band, and Hernias)

The Vixen Chronicles
(DUI: Dating Under the Influence of Some Very Bad Men)
co-authored with Brandy Pinkerman Janke

Table of Contents

Introduction

All right, the time has come. You're thinking of self-publishing a book and you're wondering what that entails. Well, you've come to the right place. This book is my sixth published, and of those, my fourth self-published. For me it's worked out well. I honestly wouldn't go back to a traditional publisher unless he or she paid me a huge, nonrefundable advance up front, and threw me a lavish book launching party that included guests like Stephen King, Neil De-Grasse Tyson, Anna Quindlen, Doris Goodwin Kearns, Jon Stewart, and that guy in my condo building with the bumper sticker on his rusted out Silverado that says "Part time organic chemist—full time Ninja." Actually, I'm only kidding. I'd do it just for the advance alone. Screw the party. But since neither a party nor an advance has been offered to me from a publisher yet, I'll continue to self-publish.

Lucky for you because each time I do it I learn something new. Plus, the technology changes (for the better, I think) and in order to stay on top of it, I have to keep pumping out books. Case in point, this is the second edition of this book since it originally came out in 2015. It's that practice-what-you-preach thing. Overall, it's a win-win situation for everyone. I have to admit, however, I never set out to become a Memoir Midwife®—which is just a funny little term I coined to describe the fact that I like to help people self-publish their books, memoir or otherwise.

In reality, your book doesn't have to be a memoir for me to get involved. I just like the alliteration.

But ironically the term Memoir Midwife® works on many levels. In my twisted universe I really do feel that being pregnant and giving birth to a child is somewhat analogous to writing a book and having it published. In both cases you go through the gestation process of building something from nothing. And then once you present that thing to the world, you have a bit of influence over it, but in the end, it pretty much goes its own way. And if that outcome exceeds everyone's expectations (even yours), well then, aren't you a genius of a parent? Or author? And if, on the other hand, it ends up being a huge disappointment, then what the hell were you thinking? The world judgmentally dubs you a goon for even trying.

But I'm getting ahead of myself. Let's get back to the point at which your project has not even been born yet. My part as your publishing coach (see, that just doesn't flow as well as "Memoir Midwife®") is not to write your book (or in other words, give birth to it) for you. But rather to supportively sit on the sidelines and yell "Breathe! Breathe! You can do it!" when the going gets tough and you just want to bash someone's face in due to the pain and frustration of trying to launch this thing out into the world. I'll calmly offer Zen-like, experiential advice and talk you down off the ledge, staying well out of reach of your flailing arms.

Another similarity is that just like there are nine months to pregnancy, there are nine steps to self-publishing your book. Coincidence? I think not. Okay, well, maybe it is a coincidence (one that I helped concoct, actually), but I like to think the Cosmos had a little something to do with it.

In 2011, I self-published my book *Confessions of a Band Geek Mom*, and as a result I was all over the media nationwide that summer, doing promotion AND talking about self-publishing. Someone from the University of Utah heard me on the radio, called me up, and asked if I'd be interested in teaching a self-publishing course as part of the university's Lifelong Learning program. I said "Sure," but then that meant I had to get organized. I realized self-publishing entailed several repetitive steps, regardless the topic of the book. So I developed a curriculum that systematically went through each of those steps. Quite by accident (and really to get things straight in my own head) I ended up taking a complicated process and breaking it down into digestible, bite-sized pieces.

My University of Utah course was a night class across multiple weeks, and every time I finished teaching it, at least one student would ask if I had a book that summarized the self-publishing steps I had just presented. I admitted I did not—mainly because self-publishing technology is a moving target and I didn't want to have to continually update my book.

But then, for the people who couldn't commit to a weekly night class, I independently created a one-day workshop (usually held on a Saturday) called "How to Self-publish Your Book." (I know—catchy title, right?) And I decided in this case, a textbook would be helpful. So I sat down and wrote brief overviews of each self-publishing step. And after several iterations, and multiple updates, that initial effort has since evolved into the book you're holding in your inquisitive, little hands right now.

As you read it, you'll notice that the chapters are very short and to the point. I purposely did that because I don't want the process to appear overwhelming, making it sound like you need an MBA and a law degree just to self-publish a book, because honestly, you don't. I try to stick to the highlights of each step, giving you just the pertinent information on an as-needed basis. And even though I occasionally offer random tips and words of caution here and there, for the most part I avoid getting bogged down in all the possible scenarios that could happen when you self-publish your book. (Trust me, you'll encounter those all on your own.)

In any case, suffice it to say after reading this you will have the basic tools and knowledge required to self-publish a book.

But just to be fair, let me share with you what you WON'T get out of this tutorial.

If you've ever taken my self-publishing class or my one-day workshop, you'll notice that this book does not include the sales and marketing aspect of my curriculum. In my class and workshop I go over a marketing plan for you to use after you self-publish your book. In fact, that's half the class. Because let's face it, you can write the best book in the world, but if no one buys it and reads it, then what's the point? But for the purposes of this book I just discuss the steps you need to self-publish a book. Period. Selling it after that is a whole other animal, which would go beyond the scope of this lesson. The first step is to get your book written and self-published. Once that's done you can tackle how you're going to get it into the collective hands of the public.

That all said, I fully admit this book simplifies a much bigger picture, not unlike those parenting tomes that prep you on what it's like to give birth. Think of this as the self-publishing version of *What to Expect When You're Expecting*. It's meant to give you an idea of what you're in for and (hopefully) provide the confidence you need to push forward.

Speaking of which, I also thought it would be fun to provide little incentives to entice you to keep going as you make your way through this book.

Just like crossing off days on a calendar when you're pregnant, I've provided a checklist at the end of each chapter, so that you can prove to yourself that you're making headway. If you're like me you like to make "to-do" lists, and there's nothing more satisfying than crossing things off your list. Why? Because a "to-do" list item with a check mark next to it or a line through it can only mean one thing—progress.

So there you have it; everything you need to know ahead of time about the nine steps required to self-publish your book. If there is any one thing I want you to remember when you use what you learn here to accomplish your own literary goals, it's this: Theory is always easier, and makes much more sense than practice. Therefore, don't get too discouraged if you run into some bumps in the road while embarking upon your own self-publishing journey. To be honest, both pregnancy and self-publishing had me tearing my hair out when I went through each the first time. And I wasn't even hormonal when I self-published my first book. (Well…not as much, anyway.) Even if something doesn't go as planned, just keep plowing forward.

And if you need a bright side on which to look, I'll throw you this bone. A book doesn't borrow your car, eat all your food, or require money for college. It also won't date a loser, call in the middle of the night begging for bail money, or throw a tantrum in the middle of Walmart. It can, however, break your heart just as easily as a son or daughter. But then again, it may not. Maybe, just maybe, self-publishing your book could be one of the most rewarding experiences of your life.

I'm here to tell you, it's worth the risk.

Write Your Book

STEP ONE

There's no getting around it. Content is king. The best way to sell a lot of books is to write the best book possible. Even if your book is not that great, or has sloppy production values, you'll still sell a few copies immediately after your book comes out. But word will soon get around that you produced a real turkey. And if that happens, all your hard work writing (and self-publishing) the darn thing quickly becomes as relevant as 8-track tapes.

That's why you can't skimp on the writing. If you're not a writer, then it's best to partner with someone who is. You can either hire a ghostwriter to pen your story for you (in which case you pay a lot of money, because the ghostwriter's name does not share author credit). OR you team up with a writing partner who knows what they're doing and you share authorship (and thus, royalties) with him or her.

The latter is cheaper, because for payment of doing the work you can split the wealth and kudos with your co-author when your book sales and all the glory come rolling in. Which means no out-of-pocket expense up front.

Typically, when you share authorship in this manner you and your co-author are listed on the cover as follows:

"YOUR BESTSELLER"
by You with Your Co-author

The "with" indicates that it's your story, but the other person wrote it for you. There's nothing wrong with that. Celebrities do it all the time when they write their memoirs. (Contrary to popular belief not just anyone can write a book.)

FORMAT

The other thing you have to do during the writing process is make sure you write your book in a program that outputs to Adobe PDF format, such as Microsoft® Word or Adobe InDesign®. In fact, I recommend you use either one of those programs. That's not to say you can't use something else, AS LONG AS it outputs cleanly to Adobe PDF without a lot of weird, hidden markup. Why? Because as we'll see later, the POD website (which stands for Print on Demand—a fancy term for a self-publishing website) typically requires that you upload the interior of your book in Adobe PDF.

Now before you get all righteous on me and claim you know of a publishing website that will let you directly upload your Apple Pages document or MS Word RTF or DOCX format, let me just say this about that: Don't do it. Here's why. Yes, some POD websites will take a non-PDF document, but then what happens is that graciously accommodating website performs the PDF conversion for you. Do you really want to risk that? Because if you do, the interior of your book may not end up looking the way you want. If, however, you upload the interior of your book as a PDF file, then what you see is what you get. A PDF is a snapshot of the modifiable desktop publishing file that is your formatted manuscript. As a result, if YOU create the PDF, then you know what the inside of your book will look like when it's printed.

If you don't know how to output your book's manuscript into a PDF file, then find someone who does and have him or her do it for you. If you have access to teenagers, they're a good choice because they're technology natives, whereas if you're over 45, then most likely you're a technology immigrant. No offense, I'm a technology immigrant, too, but I love this stuff, so I totally embrace it. Or if you don't have access to technology natives or geeks like me, then bite the bullet and hire a production designer to help you. (See Step 8—but don't actually go to Step 8 until you've read Steps 2 through 7. Let's not get too far ahead of ourselves here. Just be patient.)

CHECKLIST

- ☐ Write your book
- ☐ Write the book in a program that outputs to Adobe PDF

TIP

Having trouble getting started writing or finishing your manuscript? For motivation take a writing course. There are good ones through your local college or university community education program. However, if the problem goes deeper than just motivation, you might need some actual guidance to structure your story and bring out its message. If that's the case, I invite you to take a look at my online writing course, *7 STEPS TO TURN YOUR STORY INTO A BOOK*. For more information go to my website at *www.TheMemoirMidwife.com* or read more about it when you get to the *Wrap Up* chapter at the end of this book. Whatever you do to motivate yourself, the key is to find a way to hold yourself accountable to write on a regular basis.

* *

Start a Publishing Company

STEP TWO

It may seem like overkill to set up a publishing company, especially if you plan on writing only one book, however keeping your self-publishing expenses and revenues separate from your personal finances not only makes for easier accounting, it's a lot safer in our present world of e-commerce.

Plus, there are several things you'll want to do when you self-publish a book (which you'll see in later steps) that are easier, and safer, to accomplish through an entity.

If you already have an entity for some other business you do, you may be able to create a DBA ("doing business as") for your publishing company under that entity. However, if your present business has NOTHING to do with self-publishing, OR the topic of your book has nothing to do with your present business, you probably want to start a unique entity for your publishing company, just to keep everything separate and clean. It's totally your call. Check with your accountant or tax attorney to see what he or she thinks.

But let's assume you're starting a new entity for your publishing company.

REGISTER WITH YOUR STATE

Fill out the paperwork to establish your publishing company as an LLC or s-corp in your home state. Why? Because then you'll get a separate tax ID for your publishing company and this accomplishes two very important things:

1. Your personal money and assets are protected from any liability your self-publishing may incur. (In other words, if some jerk decides to sue you because of your book, it's easier to protect your personal assets.)

2. Tracking how much revenue you make from the sales of your book—which by law you have to report to the IRS—is much more straightforward.

This leads us to the downside of creating a separate entity; having to keep a separate set of books for your publishing company, and filing an annual corporate tax return each year you keep your publishing company open. The tax accounting and record-keeping is stricter if you are an s-corp versus an LLC, however, with the new tax laws starting in 2019, LLCs don't get as many tax breaks as they used to (check with a tax professional on this). Either way, you will have to pay one-time state government fees to set up your entity, and possibly a regular annual state fee just to keep the company going (California, for example, requires an annual franchise corporate tax fee, whether you show a profit or not). The costs vary from state to state. To be safe it's best to consult a bookkeeper, CPA, or tax attorney before you file your first return. But the good news is there is a ton of information now on the Internet about the tax repercussions of setting up an entity (no matter which state you live in), so you can do a fair amount of research yourself before you start retaining professionals.

DON'T FORGET THE FEDS...

...because they won't forget you. Once you set up an entity in your state, the Federal Government expects you do to the same with them. The Feds take it personally if you don't invite them to the party. So in addition to applying for your state tax ID, you have to do the same with the Federal Government. To do so, go to *www.irs.gov* and in the search box on the home page type: apply for new EIN ("EIN" stands for "employer identification number"), then follow the resulting links. Or better yet, if you already have access to a tax professional, have him or her do it for you.

SET UP A CORPORATE BANK ACCOUNT

I know it's tempting to simply merge your publishing revenue and expenses with your personal banking, but trust me it's safer if you don't. Not only does having a separate business bank account make general accounting and tax reporting easier, but you also don't have to give out your personal bank information to websites that use direct deposit as a means to pay you.

Like who, you may ask? Well, to name a few: your POD (there's that ominous acronym again, which stands for Print on Demand), your e-book account (assuming you publish your book to various e-readers), your audio book account (yet another source of revenue for your book), and your Square Up, or other credit-card-payment, account (you are going to accept credit cards when you sell your books yourself, right?).

Not only do you use your POD website to print your books, but it becomes your book distributor, as well. Therefore, you'll both pay your POD (to buy your books wholesale) and be paid by your POD (when it sends your books to bookstores or online customers), so money will be coming in and going out of the bank account attached to your POD website. You'll also have a similar setup for the e-book and audio book versions of your book on yet other publishing websites (depending on the e-reader and audio book platforms), and you will have an Amazon account for when your book sells directly to customers online. Plus, you'll set up a credit-card-acceptance account, like Square Up, to sell your book to customers who pay with credit cards. All these e-commerce sources will be trafficking money in and out of your bank account.

That's a lot of third-party strangers that have access to your bank account. For the most part giving your bank information to publishing vendors is completely safe. But in those rare instances when it's not, isn't it nice to know that they can't gain access to the same account you use to make your house payment or buy groceries?

CHECKLIST

- ☐ Select your small publishing company name
- ☐ Fill out all state and federal paperwork to establish your company as an entity (LLC or s-corp is best, but check with your tax professional first)
- ☐ Set up a separate bank account for your entity

TIP

Be creative when you name your publishing company. A great business name lends itself to some fun branding and marketing possibilities down the road if you're in this for the long haul. However, if you have your heart set on naming your publishing company after yourself, then go for it. There are no right or wrong ways to brand your company here, as long as you make your company name memorable. A good tagline or slogan doesn't hurt, either.

TIP

Before you commit to a company name, make sure the URL domain name is not taken, so that you can have a website that reflects your company name. Any domain hosting website (like GoDaddy, HostGator, 1&1 IONOS, etc.) can tell you if a URL name is taken, but the easiest and quickest way to find out is to go to *www. domain.com*, and type in the URL name you're inquiring about in the search box. If it's taken, a message will appear telling you so, but some second-choice options will also come up. Once you settle on your URL domain name, shop around for your hosting company and compare prices before you commit to one. Many hosting companies offer huge discounts in the first year.

TIP

Search the U.S. Trademark database (by going to *https://www.uspto.gov/trademarks-application-process/search-trademark-database*) to make sure the company name and/or slogan you intend to use is not already in use by someone else. If someone else owns (or even has registered for) the trademark to your business name or slogan, they can legally stop you from using it, no matter how much money you've already sunk into your branding.

TIP

Open a separate company for your publishing entity in your accounting software.

TIP

Don't forget, your new entity will require BOTH state and federal tax IDs.

TIP

There are many ways to accept credit cards, but my personal favorites are through PayPal, Venmo (which is owned by PayPal), and Square Up. Square Up (*www.squareup.com*) is a website that allows you to turn your smartphone or tablet into a credit card reader. That way you can accept credit cards if you unexpectedly sell a book at your kid's band concert or in the produce aisle of your local supermarket. Hey, don't scoff. It can (and will) happen.

TIP

Most banks have small business options to set up free or inexpensive accounts that include great amenities. Shop around for the best deal on business bank accounts before you commit. Your publishing bank account can be pretty basic, so you don't need to pay for a lot of pricy bells and whistles.

Copyright Your Book

STEP THREE

The old trick of mailing yourself your manuscript, and then keeping the unopened envelope locked in your bottom desk drawer will not protect your copyright. The best way to prove you own the rights to the contents of your book is to actually copyright the darn thing, which fortunately is not hard to do. In fact, it's so super simple that it's the shortest (and easiest) step in this book. But still important, nevertheless.

First go to *www.copyright.gov*, and click on the "Register a Copyright" hot button at the top of the homepage. Once you've done that, you'll be taken to the Registration Portal where you can read Frequently Asked Questions (FAQs) or log directly into the Electronic Copyright Office. If you've never been before you'll have to set up an account. After you log in, you can select the type of work you wish to copyright (i.e., literary manuscript, script, songs, poems, a collection of work, etc.) and then you're off and running. In your case, you'll pick literary manuscript, if you're copyrighting your book.

Don't worry, the process is pretty self-explanatory and the website walks you through it. In general, you answer a bunch of questions, upload your manuscript, pay your fee, and then you're done. After that you can print a certificate of copyright showing exactly when your book was copyrighted.

As of this writing, to copyright a book manuscript with one author costs $35. If you have multiple authors it will cost a little more. Be sure to click on the "Copyright Office Fees" hotlink on the website for a complete list of costs (*https://www.copyright.gov/about/fees.html*). Copyright fees were last raised on May 1, 2014, so who knows when they'll go up again? But regardless, don't let money be reason for you to procrastinate. Copyright your book today. You don't need to have the final version of your book for your copyright to be enforced. Copyrighting your first draft is good enough. (You can even copyright just a synopsis.) Then upload your manuscript document in one of several formats the copyright office accepts, which includes the old standbys—PDF, Word (doc and docx), Pages, RTF, plus a slew of others.

QUICK SIDEBAR

Depending on which blogs you read, there is a misconception running around out there that you MUST copyright your work in order for it to be protected. That's simply not true. In the United States you own the copyright to your intellectual property the second you create it. No ifs, ands, or buts about it. That includes blog posts, social media posts, magazine and newspaper articles, songs, song lyrics, paintings, graphics, sculptures, etc. Just about anything that can be artistically created.

The trick is to protect your copyright if someone claims they have rights to use and/or profit by your intellectual content. And that's where it gets messy, because you cannot copyright an idea, only a literal work. Therefore, if you told someone the plot to your story, for example, and then they ran home and wrote and published a novel that was very similar to your idea before you got around to writing your version of it, you most likely won't win a lawsuit or claim against that jerk-of-a-friend for copyright infringement, because you never created anything using that idea in the first place.

Even if you had a first draft of a novel that showed you had that exact same story plot idea first, or even if you had a treatment (which is just a brief narrative of your story), it would still be hard to go after your jerk-of-a-friend unless he copied your written work verbatim, and I mean literally published your pages as his own. And even then, you'd have to prove that you are the originator of that work.

That's when a copyright is useful. By filing your literal work with the U.S. Copyright Office, you have a record of what your intellectual content looks like at a specific point in time. You can still win a copyright claim, even if you haven't copyrighted your work, but it just makes it so much easier for you to emerge victorious if you have a copyright that conclusively shows you are the creator (and thus legal owner) of your artistic work.

CHECKLIST

☐ Go to *www.copyright.gov*

☐ Copyright your book by filling out an online form and uploading your manuscript

☐ Keep an electronic and paper copy of your certificate of copyright

TIP

There are websites out there that say they'll copyright your book for you for a fee. For the most part, this is a scam. It's so easy to copyright your book yourself that you don't need to pay someone to do it for you. Just go to *www.copyright.gov*, follow the instructions, and do it yourself. You'll be glad you did.

Buy Your Book's ISBN

STEP FOUR

ISBN stands for International Standard Book Number. Every printed book that sells in retail outlets via literary distributors has an ISBN, sometimes called the ISBN number. However, this is as redundant as ordering KFC chicken, because the 'N' in ISBN stands for "number." The ISBN is a 13-digit series of numerals that's always listed in the front of the book on the page that has all the copyright and publisher information. It's a unique number that's assigned to your book by a government or non-government agency, depending on the country. Think of your book's ISBN as the same as a social security number for a person or the VIN for a car.

You do not have to understand what every digit in an ISBN stands for in order to self-publish your book. However, if you are interested, this is how it breaks down:

In the United States the 13-digit ISBN has five parts, usually (but not always) separated by dashes, as follows:

XXX-X-XXX-XXXXX-X

The first three digits in part one is the EAN[1] or UPC number (currently either 978 or 979), which is used as part of the barcode shown on the back of your book. (We'll get to barcodes in the next step.)

---

1   EAN stands for European Article Number, and is the European form of the Universal Product Code (UPC). UPC is the barcode you see on all retail products in the United States.

The single digit in part two identifies the country of publication or language in which the book is written.

The three digits in part three is the publisher identifier (this is the number you will have to provide in your application to obtain a Library of Congress Control Number, as explained later in Step 5).

The five digits in part four identify the title or edition of your book.

The single digit in part five is the check digit, used like the parity bit in a binary number to check for errors.

In the United States ISBNs are issued by the non-government agency Bowker, and can be purchased online by going to *www.ISBN.org*. Once there you have the option to buy one ISBN or groups of them at a greatly discounted price point. How do you decide which to do? If you KNOW you'll write only one book in your entire life, then go ahead and purchase just one ISBN. As I write this, one ISBN costs $125. However, if you plan on writing more than one book, then the best deal is to buy 10 ISBNs at the low price of $295, dramatically dropping your price point to $29.50 per ISBN. ISBNs never expire, so you don't have to worry about losing your investment. The only way that will happen is if you never write another book.

After you purchase your ISBNs they are yours and yours alone. Actually, they belong to your publishing company. You cannot give your ISBNs away or share them with another author, unless you intend to be the publisher of that author's book. But if you plan only on publishing your own books, then the ISBNs you purchase on behalf of your publishing company are there for any future books you write, and no one else.

A QUICK NOTE ABOUT BOOK RIGHTS

In general, whoever owns (purchases) your book's ISBN controls the destiny and fate of your book, which in some ways is way more important than the copyright of your book. Why? Because the publishing company (remember when you set that up in Step 2?) is identified in the ISBN as the "owner" of the book for the duration that it is in print under that company's imprint. The author may still own the copyright, but the publishing company owns the right to produce, market, and distribute your book however they see fit. This means they own the book's metadata[2] and the ancillary rights. Therefore, the publisher gets to decide how the book looks, what's on the cover, how it's marketed and sold, etc. For example, if they want to create some crazy meme for your book to be passed around on social media, but you're not nuts about that idea, then too bad. They still get to do it. They don't even have to run it by you first. Until all rights revert back to you (if ever), what the publisher says, goes—UNLESS you have it in your contract to say otherwise. And if you're a new author, a publisher will most likely not let you alter their standard contract.

Then there are the ancillary rights (which the publisher also owns for the duration of their contract with you). The ancillary rights of your book are what a publisher sells to third party content providers; a film production company, for example, to turn a book into a movie; or merchandise rights to a toy company to make the book's characters into action figures; or even putting the name of the book on aprons or swanky T-shirts and

---

2 I'm not going to assume anything here. Just so we're all clear, metadata is data about data. In the case of a book, the metadata includes stuff like the author, publisher, publishing date, page count, awards the book has won, cover art, book reviews, etc. Metadata is used extensively in today's social media world for advertising and promotion, and provides the hooks search engines need to get your book circulating on the Internet.

then selling them in Nordstrom. In many cases a book's ancillary rights are worth WAY more than the copyright of a book itself. (Think about *The Lord of the Rings* trilogy or the *Harry Potter* franchise.)

So if, for example, the POD website you use to self-publish your book offers to give you your book's ISBN for free, then technically that POD company is the book's publisher (even if you've set up your own publishing company) and as such the POD company legally can make all the major aesthetic, marketing, distribution, and ancillary decisions about your book without bringing you in the loop. Would the POD company you choose exercise that right? Probably not. But do you want to take that chance? Definitely not.

To make it clear, let's look at a hypothetical scenario. After a publisher publishes your book, let's say someone reads your book and thinks, "Wow, I want to make a movie of this!" Or maybe he or she just wants to buy 100 copies of your book for a tradeshow. Regardless, that inquiring person's point of contact (regarding your book) is the publisher, not you. Even if they figure out how to contact you first, legally you have to refer them to the publisher. But let's say the inquiring person contacts the publisher and not you, and the publisher drops the ball and never gets back to that person. You'd never know, because the publisher doesn't have to tell you anything. By letting a POD company provide your book's ISBN to you for free (as opposed to you buying your own ISBN for your book) you run the risk of lost revenue, lost marketing, and even lost promotional opportunities. At the very least, you are not the official publisher of your book.

In the world of traditional publishing (where a publisher such as Random House publishes your book for you), the publisher ALWAYS provides a book's ISBN at no cost to you (the author), and thus the publisher is the legal point of contact for your book. This is not so bad, however, because Random House probably won't drop the ball if someone contacts them about your book. I say "probably" because let's face it, Random House is pretty huge, and you may not be a big enough author name for them to bother to return calls on your behalf.

That's not to say the author gets nothing if he or she goes with a traditional publisher. In a standard publishing contract, the publisher pays a small percentage to the author for each copy of the book sold (a royalty), plus gives the author an additional small one-time pay-out or ongoing percentage if the book makes any money in the ancillary markets (like if the book is made into a movie or exercises merchandising options).

That's all fine and dandy if Random House, or Penguin Books, or Scholastic Books comes knocking and throws a big fat advance your way to publish your book. However, if you go to all the trouble and expense of self-publishing, why not keep all your rights? So pony up the money and purchase your book's ISBN, making your publishing company the "official" owner of your book. That way there's no question about who decides what when Hollywood comes knocking and wants to turn your bestseller into a summer blockbuster.

AND if a big publisher sees your beautifully completed book and decides they would like to reissue your book under their imprint, well, then they can give you an attractive advance for the privilege to do so. In which case they'll assign a new ISBN to your book before reprinting it. But that's okay, because by then their check for your advance will have cleared.

CHECKLIST

☐ Go to *www.ISBN.org*
☐ Buy your book's ISBN

TIP

Like applying for a copyright, there are websites out there that will offer to get your book's ISBN for you for a fee (but still allow you retain your rights). Unless they are literally publishing your book for you, it's not worth it, because it's just too easy to go to *www.ISBN.org* and do it yourself. Save your money.

TIP

If you intend to write more than one book in your lifetime, purchase a package of 10 ISBNs, as opposed to one ISBN. It's a better price point per ISBN.

TIP

Ebooks do not require an ISBN. So if you self-publish your manuscript ONLY as an e-book, you do not need to purchase an ISBN. However, that doesn't mean you can't add an ISBN to your e-book. Why would you want to do that? So that your e-book is searchable in the ISBN database. Therefore, if you purchased a pack of 10 ISBNs, and you don't mind burning one on your e-book, then go ahead and assign a new ISBN to your e-book. Don't use the same ISBN for the e-book that you used for the print version. The print version and the e-book are two unique representations of the same literary material, and therefore are different objects in the eyes of the publishing world.

Get Your Book's Barcode

STEP FIVE

When you go to *www.ISBN.org*, you'll notice that you can also purchase barcodes. What the heck is a barcode, you ask? It's the scannable series of verticals lines (a.k.a. the UPC) you find on everything now days, from a box of diapers to a paperback copy of *Catcher in the Rye*. Here's an example of one:

A barcode has all the point-of-sale information encoded in it, including the title, author, publisher, and (most importantly) price. For any book sold online or in a bookstore, you'll find the barcode in the lower right corner of the back cover.

In almost all cases, your book has to have a barcode before any mainstream retail outlet (including *Amazon.com* and e-book online stores) will sell your book. Therefore, when you design your book cover, be sure you leave a 2" wide by 1.2" tall white box in the lower right corner of the back cover. That's where your barcode will go. The barcode has to go over a white background regardless of the background color of the rest of your book cover.

There are two ways you can get your barcode:

1. You can buy it on the *www.ISBN.org* website for $25 (or less, if you buy them in bulk)

2. You can get it for free from your POD website

Unlike the sticky wicket of rights ownership and ISBNs, there is no legal repercussion of allowing your POD to provide you a barcode for free. However, there are some pros and cons to buying your barcode as opposed to getting it for free from your POD provider. Consider the following:

THE PROS AND CODES OF BUYING YOUR BOOK'S BARCODE	
POD provides a free barcode	**You buy a barcode from ISBN.org**
PRO: You save yourself $25	**CON**: You shell out at least $25 per book
PRO: You can determine your book's price right before you publish	**CON**: You have to know your book price at the time you purchase your barcode (because the price is permanently encrypted in the barcode)
PRO: You can change your book's price after it's published without having to purchase a new barcode	**CON**: If you ever change your book's price after it's published, you have to buy a new barcode, and then reupload your book's cover to the POD
CON: A consumer can't determine a book's retail price by looking at the barcode on the back of the book	**PRO**: A consumer can read the book's retail price as part of the barcode (because it's printed numerically above the barcode)
CON: Book distributors (such as IngramSpark) will not let you create an account for your publishing company and book if it has a POD-issued barcode	**PRO**: Distributors will allow you to create an account for your publishing company and book, as long as it has an independently-issued barcode by a non-POD publisher

I used to prefer the flexibility of letting a POD provide the barcode for me, because if I wanted to change the price of my book after it was published, I could do so without getting a new barcode. Plus, allowing the POD to issue the barcode saved me a whopping $25.

But now things are different, and it's not worth the flexibility or savings. Here's why…

BOOK DISTRIBUTORS

If you want your book in retail bookstores, your book has to be sold by one of the big three book distributors; Baker & Taylor[1], IngramSpark, or Amazon. These are the warehouse companies that buy books from publishers and then store them for retailers to purchase. The distributor is the conduit between the publisher and the bookstore. Publishing houses do not sell directly to bookstores, they sell to distributors, who then sell to bookstores. It's one more level of monetary overhead that eats into the profit of a book.

Anyway, if you want your book in bookstores, then getting your book into a distributor's warehouse is a necessary evil. Some bookstores will buy books directly from self-published authors (although most won't), but given how many thousands of bookstores there are in the world, do you really want to be responsible for the fulfillment of getting your book into as many bookstores as possible? I sure don't.

It's super easy to get your book on Amazon (which I'll go over in *Step 9, Select Your POD*). But getting your book distributed by

1   In May of 2019 Baker & Taylor announced that it will discontinue the retail wholesale side of its business by the end of 2019 (see *https://www. publishersweekly.com/pw/by-topic/industry-news/bookselling/article/79933-b-t-to-close-its-retail-wholesale-business.html.*) I will address this more in Step 9 and how this affects you as an author and self-publisher, but until Baker & Taylor officially shuts down this arm of its business, Baker & Taylor is still, as of this writing, one of the big three book distributors.

a third-party distributor, like Baker & Taylor or IngramSpark, is another issue altogether. To make sure your book gets accepted by ANY third-party distributor *cleanly*, you have to purchase the barcode for your book yourself from *ISBN.org*; don't use the free one offered by your POD company. Pony up the 25 bucks and be done with it. If your book has a free, POD-issued barcode, and you try to set up an account with Baker & Taylor or IngramSpark to be your distributor, they won't accept your book, because they assume that your POD company is your publisher, and thus doing your book's distribution already for you (which is true in theory, but in reality, probably isn't the case).

Some POD companies offer an "expanded distribution" option when you set up your book for publication, claiming they'll get you into all the book distributors. And that may be true, but even if they do get your book into all the distribution outlets, you won't be able to log into those distributors to see how many books they've sold to retailers on your behalf— because you don't have accounts of your own with them. You're coming in through your POD company's account, and your POD company probably has tons of books (besides yours) on their account. Suffice it to say, your POD company isn't going to give you specific information about how many books your distribution channels have sold, at least not to the level you will want.

And in anticipation of your next question, *"Why can't I just sign up for POD expanded distribution AND individual accounts with distributors?"* the answer is you can't. Because then you'd be in the distribution company's system twice, making things REALLY confusing for everyone involved.

Therefore, the bottom line is this: go to *www.ISBN.org* and buy the barcode for your book. It will make your life easier down the road when you're trying to get your books into bookstores.

Like ISBNs you can buy barcodes in bulk and get a better price point. As I write this, one to five barcodes costs $25 each, six to 10 barcodes costs $23 each, and 11 or more barcodes costs $21 each. And if you haven't bought your ISBNs yet, you can get deals in which ISBNs and barcodes are bundled together for one price.

You can find all of this easily on *ISBN.org*.

CHECKLIST

☐ Determine the price of your book. Make sure it's a price you can live with long-term.

☐ Go to *www.ISBN.org* and buy your barcode

TIP

If you're planning on writing more than one book, buy multiple barcodes to get a better price point.

TIP

If you haven't purchased your ISBNs yet, consider purchasing one of the ISBN/barcode bundle deals on *ISBN.org*.

Lobby (the Library of) Congress

STEP SIX

The Library of Congress Control Number (LCCN) is not required for self-published books. However, like the BISAC category code (which we'll get to in Step 7), it's just one more way to get your name and book out there in the big, bad world for free, plus it adds legitimacy to your book, especially if you want librarians to pay attention to you.

Although the Library of Congress is the research library in Washington, DC, that the U.S. Congress uses, anyone can go in for free and peruse the stacks. Unlike most libraries, however, you cannot check books out of the Library of Congress. You can do research there using their books, but you can't take them out of the building.

Many people think of the Library of Congress as the U.S.'s National Library, just like the Capitol building in Washington, DC, is considered ground zero for all our nation's laws and politics. Every book in the Library of Congress is catalogued with its own, unique LCCN. A book gets only one LCCN, even if there are multiple editions of that book. Unlike ISBNs (which are re-issued every time a book is updated and reprinted as a new edition), all editions of the same book use the book's original LCCN. Many librarians nationwide use a book's LCCN to catalogue the books in their own library's collections.

Which brings us to why you want your book in the Library of Congress.

If you think about it, it's so much easier for a librarian to add a book to his or her library's collection if it's already catalogued to fit in. Otherwise, the librarian will have to retrofit your book in, which I'm sure happens all the time, but why make it hard for a library to carry your book?

Next, having an LCCN for your book adds legitimacy to the publication of your book. Every book published by traditional publishing houses (i.e., Random House, HarperCollins, Simon & Schuster, etc.) receives an LCCN. Publishers then list that LCCN in the front of their books along with the copyright year, ISBN, and publisher info. If you want your book to be considered a legitimately published book, then you should do the same.

Plus, along with your copyright and ISBN, having an LCCN means that you're catalogued with the Library of Congress (even if your book isn't physically in the Library of Congress), which adds further strength to the fact that you own the rights to this intellectual property. This can only help you if you ever find yourself ensnared in a nasty copyright infringement case that involves your book.

And finally, it's free. There is no fee to apply for an LCCN. Having an LCCN for your book is just one more way for your book to get exposure, so you might as well do it.

Also, it's important to understand that getting an LCCN for your book from the Library of Congress, and the Library of Congress actually adding your book to their physical collection, are two different things. Although almost anyone who applies will get an LCCN for their book, only about sixty percent of self-published books that apply for LCCNs are physically added to the stacks in the actual Library of Congress. You have to remember, it's a research library. So if you wrote an erotic romance novel, and you applied for an LCCN for your steamy book, you'll probably get your LCCN, but it's unlikely your book will be physically added to the Library of Congress.

IT'S GOVERNMENT, SO BE PATIENT

To get your free LCCN you start by going to the Library of Congress's PrePub Book Link (PPBL) page at *https://loc.gov/publish/prepubbooklink/* and sign up for an account. This PPBL webpage and process is a fairly new way the Library of Congress has set up for applicants to apply for LCCNs. So if you've applied for an LCCN in the past under the old Preassigned Control Number (PCN) webpage, then you need to start over (for all new books going forward) by setting up a new account under PPBL. (The Federal Government just loves acronyms, don't they?) Since you are a self-published author your approval for a new PPBL account should happen immediately. After that, you can apply for your book's LCCN by following the instructions. But do it sooner than later, because you cannot get an LCCN for your book after it has been published. Therefore, you must apply for, and receive, your LCCN before your book goes to print. And since the Library of Congress is a government agency, it takes a while in between applying for your LCCN and actually getting one. So start this process as early as possible.

To sign up for an account you have to have previously created your publishing entity and acquired your book's ISBN. In the LCCN application you will be asked for your publishing entity's name, address, phone number, and website, along with your full name (as the publisher, senior member, and contact person). You will also be asked to give the publisher identifier portion of your ISBN, which is part three of the book's ISBN, as explained earlier in Step 4.

For example, let's say your book has an ISBN of: 978-0-962-97750-6

Notice that the three digits in part 3 of the number are 962. Those three digits (962) are the publisher identifier number of your publishing company. In order to get an LCCN for your book from your publishing company, you enter those three numbers (962) in the LCCN application. It's important to note that you, as the publisher, can't get those three numbers unless you have an ISBN for your book. And you can't get an ISBN unless you have a publishing company. Do you see now how this process builds upon itself, starting with creating your own little publishing company? It's like that nursery rhyme *This is the House That Jack Built*, in which each verse is dependent upon the previous line.

Once your book has been assigned an LCCN it goes on the copyright page in the front of your book, along with the copyright, ISBN, and any other legal information you think is important to publish.

CHECKLIST

☐ Sign up for a Library of Congress account (optional, but do it anyway—it's free)
☐ Acquire an LCCN for your book
☐ Make sure you add your book's LCCN to the front matter of your book before you go to final publication

TIP

Apply for your LCCN sooner rather than later. In other words, don't wait until you're done writing. Once you've set up your entity and obtained your ISBN, the next step is to set up your Library of Congress account by filling out the PPBL page (*https://loc.gov/publish/prepubbooklink/*), as described above. You don't want to have to hold up publishing your book because you're waiting on your LCCN.

To BISAC or Not to BISAC

STEP SEVEN

Have you ever noticed that bookstore shelves are divided into topical sections? For example, there are books on *humor, science, travel, family & relationships, cooking, performing arts, law*, blah, blah, blah, the list goes on and on. In order for customers to be able to find what they want in any bookstore those sections are standardized through category codes. So how does a bookstore owner know in which section to place an unfamiliar book? All the owner has to do is look on the back at the book's BISAC code.

BISAC stands for *Book Industry Standards and Communications*, which is an offshoot of the *Book Industry Study Group* (BISG). BISG was formed in 1975 in an effort to improve book research in the U.S. by organizing all books into standardized categories. Go into any bookstore and seven out of 10 books you pull off the shelf will have a BISAC code category listed on the back of the book in the upper left corner.

For example, I put the BISAC code of "humor" on my book *Confessions of a Band Geek Mom*, because it's a collection of funny essays based upon my standup comedy. I want *Confessions of a Band Geek Mom* to sit squarely between Ellen DeGeneres's *Seriously...I'm Kidding* and Nora Ephron's *I Feel Bad About My Neck*, given books are usually alphabetized by author's last name. (This puts me in very good company on a bookstore shelf.)

Adding a BISAC code to your book cover is optional…and free. By law you don't have to have one. But if you do decide to assign a BISAC code to your book, you do it when you set up your book's account in your POD website (which we'll get to in Step 9). And since it's just one more tool available to make it easy for your readers to find you, I can't think of a reason why you wouldn't want to do it.

To see the BISAC code categories available, go to the BISAC page of the BISG website at: *https://bisg.org/page/ BISACSubjectCodes,* and click on the hot link text that says "Complete BISAC Subject Headings List" (currently, it's at the bottom of the webpage). The list of codes gets updated every few years, but they only add codes and rarely retire them, so you don't have to worry that the code you choose will be obsolete after you publish your book. For example, under SOCIAL SCIENCE there is a sub-category of LGBT, which didn't exist 20 years ago.

As of this writing, the list of BISAC codes was updated in November of 2018, and in that list you'll see these code categories:

ANTIQUES & COLLECTIBLES

ARCHITECTURE

ART

BIBLES

BIOGRAPHY & AUTOBIOGRAPHY

BODY, MIND & SPIRIT

BUSINESS & ECONOMICS

COMICS & GRAPHIC NOVELS

COMPUTERS

COOKING

CRAFTS & HOBBIES

DESIGN

DRAMA

EDUCATION

FAMILY & RELATIONSHIPS

FICTION

FOREIGN LANGUAGE STUDY

GAMES & ACTIVITIES

GARDENING

HEALTH & FITNESS

HISTORY

HOUSE & HOME

HUMOR

JUVENILE FICTION

JUVENILE NONFICTION

LANGUAGE ARTS & DISCIPLINES

LAW

LITERARY COLLECTIONS

LITERARY CRITICISM

MATHEMATICS

MEDICAL

MUSIC

NATURE

PERFORMING ARTS

PETS

PHILOSOPHY

PHOTOGRAPHY

POETRY

POLITICAL SCIENCE

PSYCHOLOGY

REFERENCE

RELIGION

SCIENCE

SELF-HELP

SOCIAL SCIENCE

SPORTS & RECREATION

STUDY AIDS

TECHNOLOGY & ENGINEERING

TRANSPORTATION

TRAVEL

TRUE CRIME

YOUNG ADULT FICTION

YOUNG ADULT NONFICTION

Picture your book sitting on a bookshelf next to your most admired competitors and then literally invite yourself right onto that bookshelf by assigning your book the same BISAC code. Otherwise, you leave it up to the bookstore owner (or worse the person who stocks the shelves) to determine where your book should go in the bookstore. If the person stocking isn't familiar with your work (and let's face it, they probably won't be) then it's anybody's guess where your book might end up.

For example, this book your reading right now has a main title of *The Memoir Midwife*®. If the person stocking the bookshelves in a bookstore doesn't read the subtitle, which is *Nine Steps to Self-Publishing Your Book* they may think that this book is about midwifing and put my book in the prenatal or pregnancy section of the bookstore, a place where NOBODY this book is intended for would ever find it. Which is why I put the BISAC code REFERENCE/WRITING in the upper left corner of the back of my book. Now it's perfectly clear to anyone stocking shelves where this book should go in the bookstore.

Which brings up another point. If you don't see the topic of your book in the master BISAC list, it may be listed as a sub-category. For example, you'll notice that WRITING or PUBLISHING or SELF-PUBLISHING are not in the BISAC master list. However, REFERENCE is there, and beneath that is a subcategory of WRITING. When I did my research to find a BISAC code for my book, *The Memoir Midwife*®, I looked at other books on self-publishing in bookstores, and found they had a BISAC code of REFERENCE/WRITING, so I used that code (REFERENCE) and sub-category (WRITING), too.

When you select your BISAC code for your book, your POD website will tell you the available sub-categories for each BISAC code. You don't have to know your code (or sub-category) ahead of time, but it helps if you do.

ADDING THE BISAC TO YOUR BOOK COVER

So how do you get the BISAC on the back cover of your book? You give it to your book cover designer and make sure that he or she includes it as part of the design. If you are one of those rare people who can actually design a professional-looking book cover yourself using something like Photoshop® or InDesign®, then it will be up to you to remember to add it to the back of your book. But more likely you'll hire someone who knows what they're doing when it comes to exterior book design. Make sure you give your designer the BISAC code early on in the process, and doublecheck that he or she knows exactly where it goes on the back cover. If you're unsure, look at how other books included a BISAC code on the back cover and then do it exactly the same way.

CHECKLIST

☐ Go to a bookstore and find the BISAC code category on books similar to yours

☐ Select your BISAC code category when you set up your book for publishing in your POD website

☐ Make sure your book designer adds the BISAC code category to the upper left corner of the back of your book

TIP

If you're not sure which category best fits your book, or if your book seems to fit in more than one category, the best thing to do is to go into a bookstore and find books that are like yours and see which BISAC category those publishers used.

Hire Professionals

STEP EIGHT

It's amazing how many people I run across who believe authors are rich. They think you write one book and instantly you're raking it in like Stephen King. Nothing could be further from the truth. The reason one writes a book is the same reason one decides to become a teacher. You do it out of passion, because you just can't help yourself. Or you do it to help advance your career by being known as an expert in your field. And how do you become an expert? By writing a book, of course.

Other than those few reasons, every other justification for writing a book pales in comparison. Money from direct book sales should NOT be your motivation. If it is, you're headed for major disappointment. However, with the advent of self-publishing there are still those who think writing a book is their ticket to immediate solvency, and that self-publishing is a free way to get there. Again, that's just crazy talk.

The reason traditional publishing houses take such a big cut of the list price of the books they produce (and the author gets a mere pittance) is because it costs a lot to turn a pile of 8 x 10 manuscript paper into a professional-looking book that can compete with all the other professional-looking books in a bookstore. Not only are there printing costs, but there are also the creative people needed to do the things the author can't do. Because let's face it, Skippy, you're just the writer.

Even if you're the best storyteller since Mark Twain, I'm willing to bet you're not the greatest when it comes to spelling, punctuation, grammar, missing words, story structure, characterization, book design, layout, artistry, or graphic arts. Not only that, I'm going out on a limb here and guessing you don't know a pig's toenail (if pig's had toes) about Photoshop®, InDesign®, Acrobat®, or Adobe® PDF files. Nor do you have any kind of relationships with professional typeset color printing companies, just in case digital printing doesn't meet your needs (which is the case if you're writing a children's picture book). Oh sure, you can buy Photoshop® and InDesign® and convince yourself that you'll master them by Tuesday, but that's a bit like putting knives in the hands of toddlers and saying, "Hey kids, hop up there on the table and carve that Thanksgiving turkey!" What you end up with is a bloody mess.

If I'm right about even one of these assumptions then you need to hire a team of professionals that can help you self-publish your book. Starting with…

EDITORS

Once you finish a first draft of your book then the real work begins, starting with editing and rewriting. I hate to be the one to break it to you, but your book is only as good as your last draft, but not quite as good as your next rewrite. I promise you, your book will NEVER feel finished, because like an artist who can't put down the brush, there's always something you think you can do to make it better.

Which is why at some point you need to turn your manuscript over to a professional editor. Not only does an editor fix all your mistakes, he or she is also able to ascertain when it's time to pry the book from your grimy, little hands and say, "Put down the pencil, Hemingway, you're done. Now let me get to work."

So who are these magical creatures that can turn your cryptic thoughts into a literary work of art?

There are two types of editors. The first is…

The Content Editor

A content editor focuses on the story structure, characters, and imagery of your book. Rather than concentrate on the technical details of the writing, a content editor focuses on flow, ensuring the story makes sense and isn't all over the map. Obviously, a content editor is more important in a fictional book, especially if the plot is twisty-turny, or the story is character-driven. But flow and structure are just as important (if not more important) if you're writing a non-fiction or "how-to" book.

For example, in the case of a narrative story, it's the job of a content editor to look for weird moments when characters do things that are, well, out of character. Or to make you (the author) aware of awkward plot points that conveniently exist only to tie up loose ends. A good content editor is worth their weight in gold because he or she makes sure that events are not contrived or that characters behave within the boundaries of the world you've created.

Many movie production companies hire story editors just to make sure that the script and characters make sense, even for documentaries. (And yet, we still have a plethora of ridiculous films with outrageous plots and unrealistic characters that would make J.R.R. Tolkien cringe. Don't even get me started.)

That's not to say a nonfiction book doesn't benefit from the *stilo rouge* of a content editor, as well. For example, if you wrote a biography you'd still want a content editor to make sure the story you've penned flows in a manner that is interesting and has a beginning, middle, and end. For example, I was hired as a content editor by the director of the documentary film *Keiko: The Untold Story of the Star of Free Willy* to make sure that the story flowed using the archival footage the director had. I pointed out a few places where I thought there were holes in the narrative, and the director filled those gaps with additional interviews. The movie came out and did quite well, landing in several notable film festivals, and can still be seen today. Hollywood knows that just because you're writing a true-to-life tale doesn't mean you still aren't telling a story. Good story structure is the key to engaging your readers, no matter what the topic or genre.

The Copyeditor

The other editor you want to employ is the copyeditor. The copyeditor checks your manuscript for technical errors, including those related to punctuation, grammar, spelling, missing and transposed words, capitalization, and a million other high school AP English topics you've long since forgotten or never learned in the first place. A copyeditor also makes suggestions on wording or warns you when something you were absolutely certain was a glimmer of literary genius goes awry—like a mixed metaphor that misses the mark.

No matter how good you think you are at proofreading you will never be able to catch all the technical or literary errors in your writing, because you're simply too close to it. So don't even try. Just bite the bullet and hire a copyeditor. In the end you'll be glad you did.

Why?

Well, put yourself on the other end of the deal. As a literary consumer, there is nothing worse than finding a bunch of typos in a book you paid good money for. And as a publisher, not only is putting out a *schlocky* product extremely unprofessional, it reflects poorly on you as a writer.

BOOK DESIGNER

Once you've written your book, then you have to figure out how you're going to package it. Several POD websites offer free book cover and interior templates, but I'm telling you right now, most of them look too cheesy and amateurish to go up against professionally published books.

If you are serious about achieving worthwhile book sales then you have to package your book in a manner that is competitive. And unless you're a professional graphic designer yourself, then you're going to have to hire a book designer to create the layout of your book.

A book designer has the artistic eye to make sure your book doesn't end up looking like a visual train wreck when everything is said and done. Through the use of color, art, placement, fonts, and general overall graphic design, your book designer comes up with a layout for your book inside and out that is both professionally and aesthetically pleasing to consumers.

Quite honestly, your book's cover is its most important asset. Because as cliché as it sounds, people actually do judge a book by its cover. Tons of research has been done on what entices people to pick up one book over another in bookstores, and trust me a professional book designer is going to know way more about these key marketing strategies than you are.

So what do you get as a result of hiring a book designer? When you're all done with the back-and-forth reviews, your book designer will give you two files that you then upload to your POD website. Those files are:

1. A single PDF file that has the front and back cover of your book

2. A single PDF file that has the formatted interior of your book

In your contract with your book designer (yes, you need to have a contract with your book designer), make sure that YOU own the cover art for your book, and not just have the rights to use it for your book. Why? Because if you only have the rights to use the cover art for your book, then that means you can't legally use any part of the cover art for other things, such as posters, T-shirts, book bags, postcards, or even crazy social media memes that you pass around on Facebook and Instagram. Plus, you want to be able to use the cover art in your branding on your website, social media, and even your official stationery. Your goal is to make sure nothing prohibits you from using any or all of your book cover art, in any form, in your advertising, promotion, and branding. And the best way to do that is to OWN the cover art for your book (all by yourself, don't share it with anyone) once you and your book designer are done working together.

Another thing you want in your contract with your designer is that you receive copies of the digital files of the final versions of both the interior and exterior of your book. In most cases, your book cover and interior will be created by your designer using programs like Photoshop® and/or InDesign®, and then saved as PDF files to upload to your POD website. Make sure you receive the final versions of your book interior and exterior files as both PDF files AND the native files of the programs that created them. For example, if your book designer created your cover in Photoshop® and your book interior in InDesign®, then make sure you receive the final Photoshop® and InDesign® files, as well as the final PDF files. Even if you don't own Photoshop® or InDesign® (or know how to use them), you still want those native files, because if you update your book later and use a different book designer, the new book designer can pick up where your previous book designer left off.

This brings up an interesting question, which is do you always have to use the same designer to design both the book interior and exterior (book cover) files for you? Not necessarily. There are designers who do only book covers and then there are designers who only do the interior design of books. And then there are those that do both. It's up to you whom you hire. There is no hard and fast rule that says a book cover designer can't do book interiors, and vice versa.

Regardless how it shakes out for you, your book designer creates those PDF files adhering to the book specifications dictated by your POD website. In a perfect world, when you upload them to your POD website, you get no error messages telling you the file format is incorrect.

Take it from someone who has struggled through the learning curve of formatting her own books' cover and interior files, versus hiring professionals to create those files right the first time. I have done the former, and from now on I will always choose the latter. I only had to do the former ONCE to realize the value of good book designers.

COSTS

Of course none of these professionals will agree to work on your book for free, but you need these people, so be prepared to shell out some cash.

How much, you ask? Well, it depends. Typically copyeditors run anywhere from $1 to $25 per page. The more pages you have for review, the price per page goes down. For example, if you have a five-page document for a copyeditor to review, they might charge you $15 per page (or more) to make it worth their while. On the other hand, if you have a 1,000-page document that you want copyedited, then they might charge $1 per page (or less), to make it worth *your* while.

Content editors charge more, with a price range anywhere from $50 to $250 per hour, depending on how much editing they must do, the value of their expertise on certain topics, and the type of project it is (book, blog, screenplay, movie, video, etc.). Typically, you can get a better price break per hour (or page) for a longer commitment and prepayment up front. For example, instead of paying $150 per hour, if you agree to pay for 10 hours up front for $1,200, then the hourly cost goes down from $150 per hour to $120 per hour.

Book designers typically quote you an estimate depending on the scope of the work, just like any other contractor. Obviously, if you hire someone to design only your book's cover, and not its interior, it will cost less than if he or she were responsible for creating the entire layout of your book, inside and out.

Suffice it to say that you are looking at a price tag of anywhere between $1,000 and multiple thousands just to design your book, especially if your book designer is subbing out some services, such as printing (if you aren't using a POD to print your book). Children's books with lots of illustrations, for example, sometimes have to be color corrected before going to digital print, or simply cannot be digitally printed in the first place. If that's the case, then the book has to be sent to an old-school, four-color printer, which adds considerably to your production cost. That's why a beautifully designed children's book like *The Very Hungry Caterpillar* costs just as much, if not more, as an 800-page hardback novel by James Michener.

The best way to approach costs with any of these publishing professionals is to map out in detail what it is you want and get it all down in a contract before you start. At a minimum, these are the things you want to agree upon:

1. A clear list of the tasks you want completed

2. A schedule, including dates and milestones, of when each task will be completed

3. The number of reviews and/or edits that go back and forth

This last one is what can quickly curdle what was once a deliciously sweet working relationship. (Okay, there's a nice mixed metaphor for you.) You can't assume that the first iteration of whatever an editor or designer gives you will be the one and only go around. Editing and production design are collaborative processes between you and your editor and/or book designer. That said, you can't expect editors and designers to make frequent changes to your project based solely on your whim ("Um…now can I see the whole thing in purple?") UNLESS you pay for it.

Try to be as proactive as possible when interacting with your publishing professionals. For example, don't employ your book designer UNTIL you have a complete draft of your book. Because every time you add or delete content it could (and probably will) dramatically change the pagination flow of your book, which means your designer will have to go back and tweak the layout to make it aesthetically pleasing. This will probably count as one of the reviews outlined in your contract. *Ka-ching!* There goes one of the steps in the process you've paid for. Don't waste them on frivolous reviews. Save those valuable interactions for final tweaking, which will happen whether you plan for it or not…so plan for it right from the get-go.

CHECKLIST

- ☐ Hire a copyeditor
- ☐ Hire a story editor
- ☐ Hire a book cover designer
- ☐ Hire a book interior designer
- ☐ Negotiate a fixed fee contract with each professional you hire

• •

TIP

Can't afford the going rate of a professional copyeditor? Consider hiring college grad students in English, Literature, or Journalism to copyedit your work. They are on their game and always looking for ways to make extra money. Put a job listing up on a college message board or check with the department head.

TIP

Need a content editor who knows about your book's subject matter? Turn to local experts first. Look for them in professional groups on LinkedIn, or check out professors at colleges and universities. And don't be afraid to contact other authors on your topic. You'll be surprised who answers your e-mails.

TIP

Just because you're technical enough, smart enough, and patient enough to suffer through figuring out how to format the layout of your book yourself, doesn't mean you should do it. Your book will look a whole lot better if you hire professionals to edit and design it.

TIP

Always have a contract (even a simple one) with the professionals you hire to help you publish your book. Make sure that you own the cover art to your book, and that you receive all the digital files (not just the PDFs, but also the native files) for the interior and exterior content of your book.

Select Your POD Website

STEP NINE

All throughout this book I've been referring to "your POD web-site" and then telling you I'll explain what that is later. Well, guess what? Later has finally come. As I've previously stated the acronym POD stands for *Print on Demand*. In a nutshell, a POD website is the place on the Internet (a website) where you upload your book's interior and exterior PDF files so they can be assembled into a book by unseen publishing elves.

Actually, it's not as mystical as it sounds, but sometimes it sure seems that way. Just as digital printing has made it easy and affordable for you to create your own business cards (with a web-site like *Vistaprint.com*, for example), digital printing has done the same for self-publishing books.

There are many POD websites that offer book printing and various degrees of publishing services, however I'm happy to narrow down the playing field for you.

In my humble opinion, which is based upon my years of experience and research up to this point, there are only two POD websites I'd consider if I were just starting out in self-publishing:

- KDP (formerly CreateSpace, owned by Amazon)

- IngramSpark

It's no coincidence that the two biggest book distributors have taken over the POD self-publishing world. If you read the first edition of *The Memoir Midwife*®: *Nine Steps to Self-publishing*

Your Book, you will recall that I recommended CreateSpace, Bookmasters, Lightning Source, Virtual Bookworm, and Lulu as viable POD platforms on which to self-publish your book. Those options were perfectly reasonable back in 2015 when my book originally came out, however things have changed a lot since then.

CREATESPACE MERGED WITH KDP (AMAZON)

To begin with, CreateSpace doesn't exist anymore. CreateSpace was Amazon's POD for self-published authors and small independent publishing houses. By far, it was the most attractive self-publishing option back in the day, because it automatically added your book to the *Amazon.com* online bookstore and Kindle Direct Publishing, also known as KDP (which creates and distributes e-books), once your book was published. This was very convenient because it eliminated several steps required by the other POD websites in order to get your book on Amazon and available on the Kindle e-reader.

But in the second half of 2018 Amazon announced that it was merging CreateSpace with KDP, which meant instead of having to have two accounts (CreateSpace and KDP) to self-publish your book, you'd now only need one (KDP) to sell both print and e-books on Amazon. By second quarter 2019 CreateSpace was gone and everything migrated over to KDP. If you have never self-published a book on CreateSpace before this means nothing to you. You get to start fresh by creating your new account on KDP, if that's the POD of your choice. However, if you had a CreateSpace account before, you had to go through a process to migrate all your CreateSpace book titles over to KDP. It was pretty painless, and if you haven't done it yourself by now, Amazon has probably done it for you.

BOOKMASTERS (BAKER & TAYLOR)

Bookmasters is owned by Baker & Taylor, under a division called BTPS (Baker & Taylor Publishing Services). That *used to* mean if you self-published your book using the Bookmasters POD website, your book would be in the Baker &Taylor retail catalogue, which means bookstores could order your book, if they use Baker & Taylor as their distributor.

That was all fine and dandy until May 1, 2019, when *Publishers Weekly* announced that "Baker & Taylor will close down its retail wholesale business in order to better align itself with the education focus of parent company Follett Corp."[1] What does that mean for current Baker & Taylor distribution clients (both publishers and bookstores)? At this point it's too soon to tell, but the *Publishers Weekly* article did go on to say that Baker & Taylor will support the retail wholesale side of its business at least through the end of summer 2019, but that the entire book distribution operation would be shut down by the end of the year.

As of this writing Baker & Taylor still plans to offer its regular POD services under BTPS—except now authors and publishers will have to find someone else to distribute their books to bookstores. And if that's the case, why bother with BTPS in the first place, when Amazon and IngramSpark offer one-stop shopping (POD and distribution)?

So as far as I'm concerned BTPS is out as a POD option.

INGRAMSPARK AND LIGHTNING SOURCE

Even though IngramSpark has been around for a while as a book distributor (as Ingram), the company got into to the POD and

1   See https://www.publishersweekly.com/pw/by-topic/industry-news/bookselling/article/79933-b-t-to-close-its-retail-wholesale-business.html

self-publishing game when it merged with the POD company Lightning Source to offer Ingram's self-publishing clients an inhouse POD option. This means that Ingram suddenly went from being just a book distributor to being a book distributor AND a POD platform for self-published authors and small independent publishers, just like Amazon.

Lightning Source started out as Lightning Printing in 1996 and was a way for independent authors and small publishing companies to affordably do a print run of their books. But now if you choose to use Lightning Source as a POD, you are invited to be an Ingram client, which is great if you want IngramSpark as your book distributor. Again, you'll still have to jump through some hoops to get your book in the *Amazon.com* online bookstore, but it's not impossible. It will just require some extra steps on your part.

LULU and VIRTUAL BOOKWORM

Now that mega giants Amazon and IngramSpark are poised to dominate the self-publishing POD arena, the other smaller POD platforms, like Lulu and Virtual Bookworm, have some major competition to contend with. To be honest, I haven't used Lulu or Virtual Bookworm in the last four years, but even so, both these smaller platforms have their own pros and cons to consider.

For example, Virtual Bookworm provides a variety of paid services, offering everything from manuscript evaluation to releasing your book in color and/or hardback, the latter of which you can't do with KDP (however, you can with Baker & Taylor or IngramSpark). The downside of Virtual Bookworm is that you have to submit your book for review before they'll publish it, and as such there is a chance Virtual Bookworm will turn down your book if they feel it's not right for them. (Amazon and

IngramSpark do not judge your content; they just print and distribute your book and leave judgment up to the general public.) But having your POD website be selective may be appealing to you, if you want your book to be distributed by a company that shares the same philosophies and level of standards that you possess (that is, if they accept your book in the first place).

Lulu, on the other hand, has some of the most competitive royalty options and free services, but the downside is their support relies quite a bit on their Community Forums. They do have a customer support number, which is great if you have a shipping question. However, I've had clients tell me that getting an answer to a specific question about their book (a design question, for example) can be challenging. To their credit, Lulu does provide video tutorials in the same vein as *Lynda.com*, however the information in their video tutorials is pretty basic stuff that you could probably figure out on your own. Therefore, if you have a hard-hitting question, or really hit a snafu, you might get frustrated trying to find the answer you need. But if you can overcome all that, and you have time to figure things out on forums and on your own, then Lulu has a lot of free or inexpensive services at your disposal. Plus, Lulu does color printing and hard cover books, as well. But again, you will have to take extra steps to get your book on Amazon, and in the Ingram catalogue.

SO HOW DO YOU PICK A POD PLATFORM?

The dirty little secret is that all POD websites pretty much do the same things, so selecting one is simply a matter of preference. Each has its own particular forté, it just depends on what's important to you.

In order to determine your POD preferences, start with research. Of course, all POD platforms will tell you that it's super simple to get your book listed in the Amazon online store and the IngramSpark catalogue, but the reality is that's not always the case, so don't make your decision based solely on what they tell you. To figure out your best POD option, determine your personal publishing path of least resistance. Ask yourself, "What are my goals for my book?" "Will I do most of the selling myself, or will most of my sales come from online?" "Do I want to make money from my book or gain niche market recognition?" Make your own list of pros and cons and then do your research to address each one BEFORE you commit to a POD platform. That way you'll end up with a POD platform that best serves the distribution and sales of your book.

For example, if color pages and a hard cover are what you need for your self-published book, then don't go with KDP (Amazon), because KDP only prints softcover books and has very limited color options for the interior of your book (and it's definitely NOT picture-book quality). If you are self-publishing a children's book, for example, that has beautiful, color illustrations on every page and you want a hard cover, then use Ingram as your POD, or find your own independent, four-color printing company to create your books and then have them ship completed books to Amazon and IngramSpark for distribution.

QUICK SIDEBAR ON CHILDREN'S PICTURE BOOKS

All self-published books are not created equal. If you're planning on self-publishing an illustrated children's book, I highly recommend you immediately get on *Amazon.com* and order the book, *Self-Publishing Your Children's Book: A Practical Guide to the Planning, Printing, and Promotion of Your Children's Book* by Katie Mullaly. Do it right now, BEFORE you go too far down that road. Self-publishing an illustrated, hard cover book is way different than creating your run-of-the-mill paperback. And it's enormously more expensive and harder to market, mainly because the printing costs make the retail price of color books higher, plus hard cover books are more expensive to ship than a box of paperbacks. You do not want to bumble your way around creating a color, hard cover book. Trust me, the mistakes are just too costly.

WHAT DOES THE POD PROCESS LOOK LIKE?

To answer this question, all I can do is share the process I use when I self-publish my books. But before I do, let me preface it by saying my way is not the be-all and end-all when it comes to selecting and using your POD platform. There are even more POD platforms out there than what I've shared. And if you've found one you like, that I haven't mentioned here, more power to you. All I'm saying is if you're new to this game and don't know any better, you have to start somewhere, so you might as well start by checking out POD websites that have been used by someone else. And since you're reading this book, that someone else is me.

Therefore, if you want to self-publish a soft cover (paperback) book, with an interior that is text only (or text, plus black and white or gray scale graphics or illustrations) then I suggest you use KDP as your POD platform (and distributor on the *Amazon.com* online bookstore) and IngramSpark as your distributor into retail, brick-and-mortar bookstores. By using KDP as your POD your book will automatically be listed in the *Amazon.com* online bookstore once it's officially published. And if you decide you want to do an e-book you can set that up using KDP, as well.

Here is what you literally do:

1. **FINISH THE MEMOIR MIDWIFE® STEPS**: Complete Steps 1 through 8 of *The Memoir Midwife®: Nine Steps to Self-Publishing Your Book*. You can actually

still be doing Step 8 (editing your manuscript and formatting your book cover and interior files) when you set up the accounts below. But you really want to make sure you've completed Steps 1 through 7 before you start opening publishing accounts. Why? Because you're going to need the information generated from doing Steps 1 though 7 in order to open your publishing accounts.

2. **SET UP A KDP ACCOUNT**: Go to the website *https://kdp.amazon.com* and set up an account for your book (it's free to do so). When you set up your account make sure that you DO NOT opt in for expanded distribution for your book. If you do, then IngramSpark will not accept your book *from you*. Accepting the expanded distribution option in KDP means that Amazon (not your publishing company) represents you and your book in the IngramSpark catalogue. And as I said earlier, if that's the case you won't get direct reports about your book from IngramSpark, because IngramSpark considers you an Amazon customer. Plus, do you really want Amazon to be the conduit between you and Amazon's biggest competitor? I think not.

3. **SET UP AN IBPA ACCOUNT**: Go to the website *https://www.ibpa-online.org* and join the Independent Book Publishers Association (IBPA). As of this writing, it costs $129 per year if you're an author/publisher. As a member you get freebies and considerable discounts on IngramSpark services, like free title setup for both print and e-books (a $49 savings), free revisions (a $25 savings), plus a slew of other benefits (go to *https://www. ibpa-online.org/page/ingramspark* for a complete list). Besides that, as an IBPA member, you have access to

a huge database of useful publishing information and training, which honestly feels like going to publishing college. It is so worth the annual subscription.

4. **SET UP AN INGRAMSPARK ACCOUNT**: Go to *https://www.ingramspark.com*, click the CREATE ACCOUNT text in the upper right corner of the homepage, open an account, and answer all the questions about you, your publishing company, and your book. There will be a monetary cost, depending on the services you select. This is where your IBPA membership comes in handy. When you check out, use the IBPA coupon code to get all your discounts and freebies. The process is pretty straightforward if you follow the directions.

That's it. Truly. Will you have questions along the way? Of course. Will you get stuck? Maybe for a second or two, but I doubt it will be a showstopper, because all the websites I list above do a great job of helping you get unstuck. Call customer support or search the Internet for answers. I guarantee you, whatever your self-publishing issue is, someone else has stumbled upon it before, and therefore the answer is out there somewhere.

CHECKLIST

☐ Complete at least Steps 1 – 7 in the book *The Memoir Midwife®: Nine Steps to Self-Publishing Your Book*

☐ Research print-on-demand (POD) websites and select one

☐ Set up your account on your POD website

☐ Join the Independent Book Publishers Association (IBPA)

☐ Set up your account on IngramSpark so brick-and-mortar bookstores can order your book

TIP

KDP allows you to make your book available on the Kindle only. But if you want your book on other e-readers, as well, then you'll need to do that outside of KDP. Go to *www.SmashWords.com* to learn more and get you book on multiple e-readers. It's important to note, however, that KDP will offer you a much bigger royalty percentage to publish your e-book exclusively on the Kindle (70% royalty versus 35%). It's up to you to decide if that exclusivity (and bigger royalty payment) works for you. For more information read the "KDP Select" portion of the KDP website.

Postpartum

Believe nothing, no matter where you read it,
Or who has said it,
Not even if I have said it,
Unless it agrees with your own reason,
And your own common sense.
  - Buddha

Creativity. If you're cursed with it it's the thing that motivates you to get up in the morning, but then bitch-slaps you down to self-loathing depths the second you try to put it to practical use. Not unlike a clandestine lover who demands all your attention, but never wants to be seen with you in public, your creativity shines brightest when you dance alone with it in the solitude of your psyche. Most of the time it reveals its beauty only to you, yet like a fool in love you spend your entire life trying to legit-imize its splendor to people who couldn't care less. Because in your heart you just know that if everyone could share the joy you feel when you craft that perfect phrase or come up with that undeniable plot twist, the world would be a much better place.

  I offer this dismal little analogy only because when you final-ly debut your great art (i.e. a manuscript, if you're a writer), and people for which you have little or no respect (or even the ones you do respect) poo-poo all over it, you can't let that deter you. I know it's hard to shake it off when someone doesn't get you, but that's all part of the creative process.

As a standup comic I've spent years (starting when I was 19 years old) publicly bearing my soul to inebriated strangers, only to be heckled or booed off the stage more often than I care to admit.

Yet I kept going.

I had to, because my creativity refused to be repressed, no matter how much I tried to smother it with the left side of my brain. Ironically constant rejection forced me to get even more creative about how I expressed my art, and at some point I realized I could choose to be either a jaded bore or a confident outcast. Admittedly I ended up embracing a little bit of both, fermenting nicely into a cynical dreamer.

When it comes to artistic feedback I always tell my kids, my students, my friends, or anyone who'll pay a nanosecond of attention to me, to do three things:

1. Listen politely (a saccharine smile on your face helps)

2. Accept what's helpful

3. Throw away the rest

There's nothing wrong with rejecting rejection. Just because someone offers you his or her opinion (solicited or otherwise) doesn't mean you have to take it. Even if they're the expert. Being a novice sometimes gives you a certain level of freedom that too much experience tends to squelch.

But if you just can't help listening to EVERYONE who coughs up an assessment of your work, including those who've never ventured an inch out on that rickety limb because they can't stomach the sound of cracking wood, simply thank them for their input and keep plowing forward. If you get lost along the way, it never hurts to use your passion as a compass.

Because if you do, you just might end up being the punch line to a gratifying success story, in which case you'll share company with the following delightfully, determined literary *losers*.

1. In 1936, Ted Geisel was a cartoonist who wrote and illustrated a children's book that he shopped around to publishers. The problem was publishers didn't want him or his silly kids' book. In less than a year, 43 publishers unceremoniously rejected Geisel's submission without offering a single word of encouragement.

   One day, while walking home to burn his manuscript out of frustration, Geisel ran into a college buddy who agreed to pull some strings in the publishing world on Geisel's behalf. Even with an endorsement, enthusiasm for Geisel's book was lukewarm at best. But finally (probably out of pity) a small publishing house called Vanguard Press decided to publish his book. As a result, *And to Think That I Saw it on Mulberry Street* debuted in 1937 under Geisel's pen name Dr. Seuss.

   No one (including Geisel) expected anything to come of it, but the book struck a chord with kids, parents, and educators. That unexpected achievement encouraged Geisel to write more, which ultimately led to a 50-year career as one of the most successful authors of children's literature of all time.

   Which makes one wonder, had that chance meeting between Geisel and his college bro not occurred, would generations of kids have missed out on *The Cat in the Hat*, *How the Grinch Stole Christmas*, *Green Eggs and Ham*, as well as countless other Dr. Seuss classics?

2. Author John Kennedy Toole wrote the critically acclaimed *A Confederacy of Dunces*, but never lived to see it published. Brilliant, but unhappy, Toole

committed suicide in 1969 at the age of 31, as a complete unknown. While going through her son's things after his death, his mother, Thelma Toole, found a smeared carbon copy of his manuscript. After reading it she decided the world needed to read it, too. Over the next 10 years she sent it to several publishers, all of which turned her away.

Relentless in her effort to get her son's manuscript published, she also repeatedly sent it to author and Loyola University, New Orleans, professor Walker Percy. Percy finally read it, just to get Thelma off his back. To his surprise, he loved the book so much he wrote a forward for it and took over Thelma's lead to champion the book.

A Confederacy of Dunces was finally published in 1980 by LSU Press. The following year John Kennedy Toole posthumously won the Pulitzer Prize for Fiction for his novel, which has since gone on to become a cult classic. (And might I add, as an author's note, it's one of my all-time, favorite books.)

3. At the turn of the 20th century author Zane Grey was actually a dentist. But he wanted to be a writer. So he set up practice in New York City just to be closer to the epicenter of the publishing world. In 1903 he finished his first novel, *Betty Zane*, and dutifully sent it out to make the rounds with all the big time, New York publishers. It was promptly rejected by everyone. So he self-published it—something unheard of in those days.

Needless to say, it didn't do that well.

Undeterred, Grey tried his hand at authorship again in 1909, this time sending his new novel, *The Last of the Plainsman*, to the same slew of publishers. Like before, they all rejected it, prompting Harper & Brothers editor Ripley Hitchcock to write to Grey: "I do not see any-thing in this to convince me that you can write either narrative or fiction."

(Ouch.)

Depressed but determined, Grey came back two years later with *Riders of the Purple Sage*. Once again Ripley Hitchcock rejected Grey's work, but this time Grey went over Hitchcock's head to the higher-ups at Harper. Someone at the top decided to take a chance on Grey. Harper & Brothers published *Riders on the Purple Sage* in 1912.

It caught fire with readers, prompting Grey to con-tinue pumping out books at a mind-boggling pace, each proving more popular than the previous. As a result, over the next 30 years Zane Grey became the 20th cen-tury's most prolific (and popular) author of cowboy and western-themed novels.

4. In 1995 J.K. (Joanne) Rowling was a broke, divorced, single, welfare mom. To escape her dismal situation she turned to writing. She wrote in cafes, coffee houses, and at home while her baby napped, all in between juggling meager jobs.

After finally finishing her first manuscript, *Harry Potter and the Philosopher's Stone*, she shopped it around to publishers on a long shot that she could turn her writing therapy into a little extra cash. To her dismay no less than 12 publishers rejected her little ditty about an orphaned boy sorcerer.

Finally after making the rounds, the British pub-lishing house Bloomsbury agreed to print Rowling's book, but it was a timid roll-out, at best. In fact, her editor advised Rowling to get a steady day job, because he didn't think she could make a living writing children's books.

Harry Potter and the Philosopher's Stone came out in the U.K. in 1997 to respectable (but not necessarily remarkable) success. To help get some of their production costs back, Bloomsbury put the U.S. publishing rights to *Harry Potter and the Philosopher's Stone* up for auction in early 1998. As luck would have it Scholastic Books won the bid for a mere $105,000 (which went to Bloomsbury, by the way, not Rowling). In September of that same year Scholastic released the book in the U.S. as *Harry Potter and the Sorcerer's Stone*. To everyone's surprise *Harry Potter* resonated with young American readers so much so that book sales skyrocketed by Christmas of that same year, and kept soaring into 1999.

In short order, Scholastic commissioned Rowling to write a sequel…and then another…and then another… spawning a total of eight more *Harry Potter* books, each more mega popular than the last.

Two decades later the *Harry Potter* series has the proud distinction of being the highest grossing children's books and movie franchise of all time. Proving that yes, Ms. Rowling can, in fact, make a decent living as an author of children's books.

5. In the 1980s John Grisham decided to write a legal suspense thriller during his public transportation commute to and from work. As one might guess, he was a lawyer back then, and as lawyers tend to do, Grisham wrote often in his job.

But mostly not the type of writing he was passionate about. So he used the dead time on the commuter train to work out his repressed creativity. The result of his literary commute produced *A Time to Kill*, John Grisham's very first novel. He sent his manuscript to countless publishers and every one of them passed on it. Finally, a small New York publishing company, Wynwood Press, decided to take a chance on him—but not too big of a chance. They printed only 5,000 copies of *A Time to Kill*, which pretty much says, "We believe in you, just not that much."

However, Grisham kept writing and after his subsequent books took off (*The Firm*, *The Pelican Brief*, and *The Client*) Doubleday bought the rights to *A Time to Kill* and re-issued it in hardback. By then Grisham was so popular with his readers that the reissue of *A Time to Kill* prompted huge book sales, and a 1999 Hollywood movie (of the same name) starring Matthew McConaughey and Sandra Bullock.

These examples illustrate that for some writers failure is simply a bump on the road to success."

Acknowledgments

Every time I publish something my list of gratitude gets longer and longer, which is a true testament to the fact that no one travels the road to success alone. For this particular endeavor I'd like to start by thanking Mandy Self and Polly Drolett at the University of Utah Lifelong Learning department. I believe it was Mandy who called me out of the blue after hearing me on the radio promoting my humor book, *Confessions of a Band Geek Mom*, which I had self-published, and asked if I'd be interested in teaching self-publishing. That phone call led to a whole new career path for me that I didn't know existed. Without my class forcing me to constantly raise the bar I wouldn't even have thought to write this book.

Which leads me to thank my self-publishing students. By now there are literally hundreds of you running around out there. This book, and everything that goes with it, all started with you and your desire to tell your story. You keep me on my toes with your expectations and your hopes. I commend you for dreaming big, and I'm flattered that you trust me to help you find your voice and share it with the world.

I'd also like to thank Kirsten Henry Fox for meeting me every Wednesday morning at Atticus Coffee and Teahouse back in the day to mentor me in business planning. I can't tell you how much I appreciate your time, expertise, and friendship. Your encouragement to write this book, and then show me how it all fits into a bigger picture, has been a priceless source of ongoing motivation. Look at me now, right? Second edition, check. Comedy career, check. Pursuing dreams, double check. I don't think you realize what a big help you've been and how important our meetings were to me (so I'm telling you).

And to Katie Mullaly, you are a source of inspiration and support that most people never get to experience in a lifetime. I am so lucky our paths have crossed. Several of my clients know Katie, because she is the owner/operator and publisher of Surrogate Press®, which publishes many of my clients' books. Katie is also the author of the popular children's book series *Land of...* (check it out on Amazon). She started out as a client, but found she loved publishing so much that she started her own company and now offers publishing services to other authors, including me! Thank you, Katie, for trusting me to guide you, so you can now guide me.

And finally to my "Wimmens" in Park City and San Diego, thank you for always being supportive at just the right times. When the proverbial excrement hits the fan I never have to bring you up to speed. You just flip into overdrive and stuff gets done. You know who you are and what I'm talking about. 'Nuff said.

About the Author

A native west-coaster, Stacy started her professional storytelling career as a standup comic at age 19 when she did an open mic night at a comedy club in San Francisco. After that she spent many nights onstage making people laugh. Three years later she graduated from University of California, Berkeley, with a mathematics degree, and became a technical trainer and sales support engineer for companies like McDonnell Douglas, Computer Associates, Arthur Andersen, IBM, Hewlett Packard, and Adobe. By day she honed her corporate speaking skills, but at night she continued doing standup in clubs like The Comedy Store, The Improv, and countless small clubs around the country. She was also a member of the improv groups The Fault Line Players and Off the Top Comedy.

Later she enrolled in the UCLA post graduate Screenwriter Certificate Program, and then found her niche as a script doctor and feature film writer. Today she owns her own story development business, branded as The Memoir Midwife®, in which she helps everyone from filmmakers to retirees find, write, and share their stories in the form of books and movies (and she still performs standup).

Stacy's writing and self-publishing workshops have become so popular that she now teaches them everywhere from private residences to corporate boardrooms. Plus, she has a popular story development online course called *7 Steps to Turn Your Story*

Into a Book, in which she uses her Story Mapping Method to help people structure their stories. You can learn more about Stacy's *7 Steps to Turn Your Story Into a Book* program in the *Wrap Up* chapter at the end of this book, or go to her website at *www.TheMemoirMidwife.com.*

As a professional storyteller, Stacy regularly performs stand-up comedy in Los Angeles, and is working on a 70-minute comedy special entitled A BIT MUCH, which recently had sold-out shows in the 2019 Hollywood Fringe Festival, winning a Producers Encore Award. She's also done a TEDx talk entitled *Prison: A Startling Path to Creativity*, which you can watch on YouTube.

To inquire about Stacy's self-publishing and writing workshops, or to book her as a speaker, please visit *www. TheMemoirMidwife.com* or e-mail her at *info@stacydymalski.com.*

Contact Stacy

As I mention in the *Wrap Up* chapter, you can always e-mail me at *info@stacydymalski.com*. I'm actually one of those rare people that will e-mail you back. Go figure.

There are other ways we can stay in contact, as well. If you're inclined to work the social media circuit, you can find me on any one of the following:

Follow me on Facebook at:
https://www.facebook.com/pg/StacyDymalskiEntertainment

Follow me on Instagram at:
https://www.instagram.com/stacy_dymalski

Follow me on Twitter at: *@StacyWriteNow*

Connect with me on LinkedIn at:
www.linkedin.com/in/stacydymalski/

Subscribe to my newsletter by signing up at:
www.TheMemoirMidwife.com.

Whew! That's a lot, I know. You don't have to do them all, just pick one that suits you best.

Wrap Up

Well, that's it. I hope you enjoyed my book! And that you got out of it what you were looking for, or at least you learned something that will help you successfully get you where you want to be.

As I mentioned in the *Introduction*, this book is not the be-all and end-all when it comes to self-publishing. It's just meant to push you out of the nest so that you can eventually fly on your own when it comes to getting your book out into the world.

However, if you do need more help, I offer several levels of service, both free and paid, that can help you grow as a writer.

If you are still in the writing or editing process of your story, and you need some guidance when it comes to story structure and flow (in other words, how to put your story together so that you get the most engagement from your readers), then I have the program for you. It's called *7 Steps to Turn Your Story Into a Book*, and it's designed to help you write a first draft of your book (or a solid rewrite if you already have a draft) even if you don't consider yourself a writer—even if you've never written anything! Focusing on story structure, the steps are lessons that systematically prepare you to sit down and write, or rewrite, and add flow and structure to your story. After taking this course, you'll know what it takes to start a manuscript or rewrite an existing manuscript so that it has a solid beginning, middle, and end, plus a message that gets to the heart of your story. All of which gets you that much closer to finishing your book.

I know not everyone who wants to write a book can afford to hire a private story consultant, which is why I've taken my story development process that I use with my private clients and created *7 Steps to Turn Your Story Into a Book*, an affordable online program that teaches you how to structure your story and write it from beginning to end. To accommodate your lifestyle and budget, I offer it in four "flavors" listed on the next page.

To learn more about these programs, feel free to visit my website at *www.TheMemoirMidwife.com*. And if you sign up for the online workshop or the online course, use the discount code MMBOOK2019 at checkout and receive 25% off the list price. You'll see that's a substantial discount. Yes, you heard that right, 25% OFF. See? This book has already paid for itself many times over. The key when you're stuck writing is to get the help you need to get unstuck. Rarely can you get unstuck all by yourself. I want to help you, and this is my way of doing so and thanking you for taking the time to read my book.

Or if you simply have a question about writing or self-publishing your book, you can contact me directly at *info@ stacydymalski.com*. Yes, it's really that simple. I promise I will e-mail you back.

Also, if you like to laugh, check out my humor book, *Confessions of a Band Geek Mom: How My Life as a Standup Comic Prepared Me for Motherhood*. It's the story of how I got into comedy and then had to balance it with motherhood once I had a couple of kids. Thankfully, those kids are grown and functioning adults, so being raised by a comedian somehow worked out for them. *Confessions of a Band Geek Mom* is available on *Amazon.com*, and is available on the Kindle, including the Kindle Lending Library.

Levels of support for The Memoir Midwife®'s
7 STEPS TO TURN YOUR STORY INTO A BOOK program

Options	Live or Recorded	Time Commitment	Free or Paid	Benefits	Student Type
Webinar	Recorded	34 minutes	FREE	Great overview of how to develop your story into a book manuscript. Can watch on demand, and repeatedly.	For the student who just wants to know what it entails to develop a story and write a book. (No interaction with instructor.)
Online workshop	Live	2 hours	Paid	More in-depth than the webinar, this is a live, online class with Stacy during which she presents her Story Mapping Method development process. Students can ask questions and get immediate answers.	For the student who wants live interaction with an instructor and answers to specific questions.
Online course	Recorded and Live	7 weeks	Paid	Walks you through each Story Mapping Method development step using your own story in the exercises. By the end of the course, your story is fully developed.	For the student ready to sit down and write their book. (One hour of consultation with instructor at the end of the course.)
Private one-on-one coaching	Live	Ongoing	Paid	Instructor personally coaches you in the development and writing of your story every step of the way. Great for students who have a partial or complete first draft and are ready for a solid rewrite.	For the student that prefers personal, hands-on coaching at any step in the writing and development process of their story.

And finally, if you enjoyed reading *The Memoir Midwife*®: *Nine Steps to Self-publishing Your Book (Second Edition)* I would sincerely appreciate it if you left a review of it on *Amazon.com*. If you didn't enjoy it, I (equally) sincerely apologize and instead of leaving a bad review, please feel free to contact me and tell me why. I'm always looking to improve and if you could help me do that, it not only benefits me, but my future students, as well.

And even if you never do any of this, I just want to say thanks for buying and reading my book. I hope it helps you get to where you want to go, wherever that may be. I'm just flattered you took the time to read something I wrote. Without readers, writers are simply shouting into darkness. Thanks for being my light.

Good luck with all your future endeavors. And if you become super rich and famous someday due to your fabulous career as a bestselling author, please remember us little people... because we're the ones who buy your books.

Write Your Book

Start a Publishing Company

Copyright Your Book

Buy Your Book's ISBN

Get Your Barcode

Lobby (the Library of) Congress

To BISAC or Not to BISAC

Hire Professionals

Select Your POD Website

Made in the USA
San Bernardino, CA
15 September 2019